1. In which city did Anne Frank hide from the Nazis?

    A. Berlin

    B. Paris

    C. Warsaw

    D. Amsterdam

2. Which Philosopher tutored Alexander the Great?

    A. Plato

    B. Isocrates

    C. Ptolemy

    D. Aristotle

3. What does the word Matrix mean in the Bible?

    A. Womb

    B. Burial place

    C. Heaven

    D. Prophet

4. Who discovered Australia?

    A. Christopher Columbus

    B. Robert Scott

    C. James Cook

    D. James Peterson

5. Saskatchewan is a province of which country?

    A. Iceland
    B. Russia
    C. Finland
    D. Canada

6. How many countries have names that end in -stan?

    A. 10
    B. 5
    C. 8
    D. 7

7. How would you write the number 5 in binary code?

    A. 1
    B. 11
    C. 101
    D. 111

8. What was the name of Alexander the Great's horse?

    A. Alexander II
    B. Achilles
    C. Bucephalus
    D. Patrocles

9. How many noses does a slug have?

    A. Two
    B. Three
    C. None
    D. Four

10. Copper and tin can be combined to make which metal alloy?

    A. brass
    B. bronze
    C. gold
    D. pewter

11. How many countries border china?

    A. 10
    B. 8
    C. 14
    D. 19

12. On which ship did Charles Darwin make his famous expedition?

    A. HMS Barnacle
    B. HMS Brave One
    C. HMS Beagle
    D. HMS Blue Whale

13. What country won the very first FIFA World Cup in 1930?

    A. Uruguay
    B. Italy
    C. Brazil
    D. England

14. Which of the following lengths is smallest?

    A. 1 micrometer
    B. 1 millimeter
    C. 1 nanometer
    D. 1 picometer

15. Which fruit floats because 25% of its volume is air?

    A. Pomegranate
    B. Honeydew
    C. Strawberry
    D. Apple

16. Which is the world's fastest animal on land?

    A. cheetah
    B. leopard
    C. jackrabbit
    D. springbok

17. Who wrote Frankenstein?

   A. Mary Shelley
   B. Percy Shelley
   C. Franklin Stein
   D. Howard Young

18. Fidel Castro was the leader of which country?

   A. Porto Rico
   B. Mexico
   C. Brazil
   D. Cuba

19. Which of these elements is not found in ethanol (alcohol)

   A. carbon
   B. hydrogen
   C. nitrogen
   D. oxygen

20. What did Rudolf Abel do?

   A. General
   B. Soviet Spy
   C. Commander
   D. Leader of the Soviet Union

21. What color is the spot in the middle of the Japanese flag?

    A. red
    B. pink
    C. blue
    D. black

22. Which city was Beethoven born in?

    A. Bonn
    B. Berlin
    C. Munich
    D. Warsaw

23. What is the capital of Finland?

    A. Oslo
    B. Oulu
    C. Vaasa
    D. Helsinki

24. In Alaska it's legal to shoot bears but illegal to do what?

    A. Scare one
    B. Chase one
    C. Yell at one
    D. Wake one up

25. Which is the nearest galaxy to the Milky Way?

   A. Andromeda
   B. Bode's
   C. Circinus
   D. Medusa

26. Which among these countries do not use the metric system?

   A. England
   B. Liberia
   C. Germany
   D. South Sudan

27. Why are hockey pucks frozen before a game?

   A. To prevent their breaking up
   B. To prevent them from bouncing
   C. To add strength
   D. To prevent injuries to players

28. What is mass divided by volume?

   A. density
   B. force
   C. speed
   D. weight

29. What country produced the most strawberries in 2016?

    A. USA

    B. Mexico

    C. Brazil

    D. China

30. What is the tallest breed of dog in the world?

    A. Scottish Deerhound

    B. The Great Dane

    C. Saint Bernard

    D. English Mastiff

31. In what city is The Parthenon located?

    A. Patras

    B. Kavala

    C. Volos

    D. Athens

32. Among land animals what species has the largest eyes?

    A. Ostrich

    B. Lions

    C. Elephants

    D. Komodo Dragons

33. In Swedish a skvader is a rabbit with what unusual feature?

    A. Wings
    B. Canine teeth
    C. Blue eyes
    D. No tail

34. How did Alexander the Great die?

    A. Illness
    B. Killed in battle
    C. Accident
    D. Murdered

35. In which city is the White House located?

    A. New York
    B. San Francisco
    C. Los Angeles
    D. Washington D.C.

36. Which is the heaviest living bird species?

    A. emu
    B. penguin
    C. ostrich
    D. rhea

37. What is the number one seller at Walmart?

    A. Toilet paper
    B. Bananas
    C. Socks
    D. Greeting Cards

38. Which U.S. President was the first to ride in a Helicopter?

    A. Eisenhower
    B. Kennedy
    C. Roosevelt
    D. Truman

39. What is the fastest growing body tissue?

    A. bone marrow
    B. fingernails
    C. hair
    D. skin

40. What was the first name of the first human in space?

    A. Vladimir
    B. Tom
    C. Joseph
    D. Yuri

41. Which of these creatures is an amphibian?

    A. agouti
    B. horny toad
    C. iguana
    D. mountain chicken

42. Which civilization invented the wheel?

    A. Egypt
    B. China
    C. Rome
    D. Mesopotamia

43. Louis Pasteur is credited with the discovery of what?

    A. DNA
    B. pasteurization
    C. penicillin
    D. x-rays

44. Which country had a personal union with Denmark?

    A. Norway
    B. Finland
    C. Iceland
    D. Italy

45. How many times was Dr. Seuss's first book rejected?

A. 27

B. 30

C. 1

D. 10

46. How many Theses did Martine Luther write?

A. 99

B. 100

C. 90

D. 95

47. Which country has the longest coastline?

A. Canada

B. Kuwait

C. Guam

D. India

48. How many popes did Michelangelo create artworks for?

A. 10

B. 4

C. 6

D. 9

49. The longest cave system is located in which country?

    A. Russia

    B. USA

    C. China

    D. India

50. Other than a General what was Stonewall Jackson other career?

    A. Carpentry

    B. lawyer

    C. teacher

    D. merchant

51. How did Marie Antoinette die?

    A. Accident

    B. drowning

    C. illness

    D. beheaded

52. Which dinosaur had 15 horns?

    A. Koreaceratops

    B. Kosmoceratops

    C. Pachyrhinosaurus

    D. Protoceratops

53. A pangolin is a type of what?

    A. amphibian
    B. fish
    C. mammal
    D. reptile

54. Where is the Sagrada Familia located?

    A. Barcelona
    B. Madrid
    C. Paris
    D. Berlin

55. The Ring of Fire is located in which ocean?

    A. Indian
    B. Atlantic
    C. Pacific
    D. Arctic

56. Which country has a flag with only two colors?

    A. India
    B. Italy
    C. Germany
    D. Nigeria

57. Which is the longest bone in the human body?

    A. femur
    B. fibula
    C. sternum
    D. tibia

58. Which country has the most number of UNESCO Heritage Sites?

    A. India
    B. Italy
    C. England
    D. Germany

59. Which country is closest to the Great Barrier Reef?

    A. USA
    B. Australia
    C. India
    D. Canada

60. How many signs are there in the Zodiac?

    A. 10
    B. 12
    C. 8
    D. 14

61. The metamorphism of limestone forms what substance?

   A. chalk
   B. diamond
   C. graphite
   D. marble

62. What is the world's biggest island?

   A. Borneo
   B. Madagascar
   C. Greenland
   D. Victoria Island

63. Which nation did Japan have colonial rule over?

   A. China
   B. Vietnam
   C. Singapore
   D. Korea

64. What country was formerly called Ceylon?

   A. Tanzania
   B. Sri Lanka
   C. Haiti
   D. Canada

65. In what month does Russia celebrate the October Revolution?

    A. November

    B. December

    C. September

    D. October

66. Oncology refers to the study of what disease?

    A. cancer

    B. dementia

    C. diabetes

    D. heart disease

67. A Malagasy lives in which country?

    A. Mali

    B. Malta

    C. Madagascar

    D. Maldives

68. In Minnesota it is illegal to tease what type of animal?

    A. Squirrels

    B. Skunks

    C. Raccoons

    D. Bears

69. What type of rock is limestone?

    A. igneous
    B. metamorphic
    C. molten
    D. sedimentary

70. Which among these countries has a non-rectangular flag?

    A. Hungary
    B. Sudan
    C. Zambia
    D. Nepal

71. Which is the brightest planet as seen from earth?

    A. Jupiter
    B. Mars
    C. Saturn
    D. Venus

72. Which WWI battle had the worst casualties?

    A. Verdun
    B. Vimy Ridge
    C. Somme
    D. Marne

73. Which basketball player appeared in the 2015 film Trainwreck?

    A. LeBron James
    B. Wilt Chamberlain
    C. Kevin Durant
    D. Michael Jordan

74. Which of these is not a type of quark?

    A. charm
    B. down
    C. round
    D. up

75. Which is the world's highest waterfall?

    A. Kunchikal Falls
    B. Ribbon Fall
    C. Angel Falls
    D. Yosemite Falls

76. What is the most linguistically diverse country in the world?

    A. Papua New Guinea
    B. USA
    C. Australia
    D. Ireland

77. What did the Olympics used to award medals for?

    A. Art
    B. Singing
    C. Writing
    D. Speaking

78. How long does it take for light from the sun to reach the earth?

    A. 2 seconds
    B. 8 seconds
    C. 8 minutes
    D. 20 minutes

79. What is Japanese sake made from?

    A. Soy
    B. Barley
    C. Rice
    D. Wheat

80. Which of the following numbers is a prime number?

    A. 6
    B. 9
    C. 13
    D. 15

81. A joule is a measurement of what?

    A. energy
    B. force
    C. mass
    D. speed

82. Who is this boxer who lost 31of his 32 bouts via knockout?

    A. Harold Brazier
    B. Eric Crumble
    C. Antwun Echols
    D. Bennie Briscoe

83. Who is the only player in NBA history to play 22 seasons?

    A. Robert Parish
    B. Kareem Abdul-Jabbar
    C. Kevin Willis
    D. Vince Carter

84. Which kind of bulbs were once exchanged as a form of currency?

    A. Daffodils
    B. Amaryllis
    C. Tulips
    D. Aliums

85. Who was the first performer at the Woodstock festival in 1969?

    A. Joan Baez
    B. Richie Havens
    C. Joe Cocker
    D. Santana

86. What year did women get the right to vote in the U.S?

    A. 1920
    B. 1919
    C. 1918
    D. 1921

87. What country won the Eurovision Song Contest 2017?

    A. Spain
    B. Portugal
    C. Croatia
    D. Sweden

88. Which country is the largest producer of vanilla?

    A. Zimbabwe
    B. South Africa
    C. Sri Lanka
    D. Madagascar

89. Who was the founder of Rome?

    A. Augustus
    B. Romulus
    C. Remus
    D. Caesar

90. How would you write the number 54 in roman numerals?

    A. LIV
    B. LVI
    C. XXXXIV
    D. XXXXIIII

91. Amino acids are the building blocks of which molecules?

    A. carbohydrates
    B. lipids
    C. proteins
    D. sugars

92. What is the capital of Qatar?

    A. Dukhan
    B. Doha
    C. Abu Dhabi
    D. Dubai

93. Which ancient society had 8-day weeks?

    A. Roman
    B. Greek
    C. Egyptian
    D. Babylonian

94. Which 1998 Disney film was Lindsay Lohan's film debut?

    A. Freaky Friday
    B. Parent Trap
    C. Mean Girls
    D. Just My Luck

95. Which country is the biggest?

    A. India
    B. Japan
    C. Thailand
    D. Singapore

96. What is dendrochronology?

    A. climate science
    B. study of skin
    C. study of teeth
    D. tree-ring dating

97. Which U.S. President had a pet parrot?

    A. Jackson
    B. Wilson
    C. Adams
    D. Lincoln

98. Where would you find cellulose?

    A. blood cells
    B. plant tissue
    C. rocks
    D. space

99. What is the only king in a deck of cards without a moustache?

    A. King of spades
    B. King of hearts
    C. King of diamonds
    D. King of clubs

100. Which is the main substance used to make a crayon?

    A. Dye
    B. Wax
    C. Plastic
    D. Chalk

1. In which city did Anne Frank hide from the Nazis?

   Amsterdam

2. Which Philosopher tutored Alexander the Great?

   Aristotle

3. What does the word Matrix mean in the Bible?

   Womb

4. Who discovered Australia?

   James Cook

5. Saskatchewan is a province of which country?

   Canada

6. How many countries have names that end in -stan?

   7

7. How would you write the number 5 in binary code?

   101

8. What was the name of Alexander the Great's horse?

   Bucephalus

9. How many noses does a slug have?

Four

10. Copper and tin can be combined to make which metal alloy?

Bronze

11. How many countries border china?

14

12. On which ship did Charles Darwin make his famous expedition?

HMS Beagle

13. What country won the very first FIFA World Cup in 1930?

Uruguay

14. Which of the following lengths is smallest?

1 picometer

15. Which fruit floats because 25% of its volume is air?

Apple

16. Which is the world's fastest animal on land?

Cheetah

17. Who wrote Frankenstein?

Mary Shelley

18. Fidel Castro was the leader of which country?

Cuba

19. Which of these elements is not found in ethanol (alcohol)

Nitrogen

20. What did Rudolf Abel do?

Soviet Spy

21. What color is the spot in the middle of the Japanese flag?

red□

22. Which city was Beethoven born in?

Bonn

23. What is the capital of Finland?

Helsinki

24. In Alaska it's legal to shoot bears but illegal to do what?

Wake one up

25. Which is the nearest galaxy to the Milky Way?

Andromeda

26. Which among these countries do not use the metric system?

Liberia

27. Why are hockey pucks frozen before a game?

To prevent them from bouncing

28. What is mass divided by volume?

Density

29. What country produced the most strawberries in 2016?

China

30. What is the tallest breed of dog in the world?

The Great Dane

31. In what city is The Parthenon located?

Athens

32. Among land animals what species has the largest eyes?

Ostrich

33. In Swedish a skvader is a rabbit with what unusual feature?

Wings

34. How did Alexander the Great die?

Illness

35. In which city is the White House located?

Washington D.C.

36. Which is the heaviest living bird species?

Ostrich

37. What is the number one seller at Walmart?

Bananas

38. Which U.S. President was the first to ride in a Helicopter?

Eisenhower

39. What is the fastest growing body tissue?

Bone marrow

40. What was the first name of the first human in space?

Yuri

41. Which of these creatures is an amphibian?

Mountain chicken

42. Which civilization invented the wheel?

Mesopotamia

43. Louis Pasteur is credited with the discovery of what?

Pasteurization

44. Which country had a personal union with Denmark?

Iceland

45. How many times was Dr. Seuss's first book rejected?

27

46. How many Theses did Martine Luther write?

95

47. Which country has the longest coastline?

Canada

48. How many popes did Michelangelo create artworks for?

9

49. The longest cave system is located in which country?

USA

50. Other than a General what was Stonewall Jackson other career?

teacher

51. How did Marie Antoinette die?

beheaded

52. Which dinosaur had 15 horns?

Kosmoceratops

53. A pangolin is a type of what?

Mammal

54. Where is the Sagrada Familia located?

Barcelona

55. The Ring of Fire is located in which ocean?

Pacific

56. Which country has a flag with only two colors?

Nigeria

57. Which is the longest bone in the human body?

Femur

58. Which country has the most number of UNESCO Heritage Sites?

Italy

59. Which country is closest to the Great Barrier Reef?

Australia

60. How many signs are there in the Zodiac?

12

61. The metamorphism of limestone forms what substance?

Marble

62. What is the world's biggest island?

Greenland

63. Which nation did Japan have colonial rule over?

Korea

64. What country was formerly called Ceylon?

Sri Lanka

65. In what month does Russia celebrate the October Revolution?

November

66. Oncology refers to the study of what disease?

Cancer

67. A Malagasy lives in which country?

Madagascar

68. In Minnesota it is illegal to tease what type of animal?

Skunks

69. What type of rock is limestone?

Sedimentary

70. Which among these countries has a non-rectangular flag?

Nepal

71. Which is the brightest planet as seen from earth?

Venus

72. Which WWI battle had the worst casualties?

Somme

73. Which basketball player appeared in the 2015 film Trainwreck?

LeBron James

74. Which of these is not a type of quark?

Round

75. Which is the world's highest waterfall?

Angel Falls

76. What is the most linguistically diverse country in the world?

Papua New Guinea

77. What did the Olympics used to award medals for?

Art

78. How long does it take for light from the sun to reach the earth?

8 minutes

79. What is Japanese sake made from?

Rice

80. Which of the following numbers is a prime number?

13

81. A joule is a measurement of what?

Energy

82. Who is this boxer who lost 31of his 32 bouts via knockout?

Eric Crumble

83. Who is the only player in NBA history to play 22 seasons?

Vince Carter

84. Which kind of bulbs were once exchanged as a form of currency?

Tulips

85. Who was the first performer at the Woodstock festival in 1969?

Richie Havens

86. What year did women get the right to vote in the U.S?

1920

87. What country won the Eurovision Song Contest 2017?

Portugal

88. Which country is the largest producer of vanilla?

Madagascar

89. Who was the founder of Rome?

Romulus

90. How would you write the number 54 in roman numerals?

LIV

91. Amino acids are the building blocks of which molecules?

Proteins

92. What is the capital of Qatar?

Doha

93. Which ancient society had 8-day weeks?

Roman

94. Which 1998 Disney film was Lindsay Lohan's film debut?

Parent Trap

95. Which country is the biggest?

India

96. What is dendrochronology?

Tree-ring dating

97. Which U.S. President had a pet parrot?

Jackson

98. Where would you find cellulose?

Plant tissue

99. What is the only king in a deck of cards without a moustache?

King of hearts

100. Which is the main substance used to make a crayon?

Wax

In New Delhi, if a tree falls sick, an ambulance is dispatched to treat them. This came into effect in 2009 and takes four people to do the job.

You can plant a pineapple by slicing off the top and planting it in the soil.

Chocolate ice cream has been proven to significantly reduce emotional and physical pain.

A Greek-Canadian man invented the "Hawaiian" pizza.

If a Polar Bear and a Grizzly Bear mate, their offspring is called a "Pizzy Bear".

There's a town in the Oklahoma panhandle named "Hooker" and its slogan is "it's a location, not a vocation".

Young Tyrannosaurus rex's probably had a thin coat of downy feathers to stay warm. They did not need them as they got older due to their size.

The length of an elephant is the same as the tongue of a blue whale.

The only letter that doesn't appear on the periodic table is J.

Approximately 1,000,000 dogs in the U.S. are named as the heirs of their owners' wills.

Iceland has a dating app that stops you hooking up with your cousin.

Alfred Hitchcock didn't have a bellybutton.

In the Philippines, you can buy spaghetti at McDonald's, where they also sell a "McDo" piece of chicken.

Ed Sheeran has a ketchup bottle tattooed on his arm.

LegoLand Billund opened on the 7th June 1968, and attracted over 3,000 visitors on the first day!

Tutankhamun's parents were brother and sister.

Cold showers have more health benefits than hot or warm showers. These include improving circulation, stimulating weight loss, and easing depression.

Only primates, humans, and opossums have opposable thumbs. Out of these, the opossum is the only one with no thumbnail.

A cluster of bananas is called a "hand". Along that theme, a single banana is called a "finger".

Females are better at distinguishing colors, while males excel at tracking fast moving objects and discerning detail from a distance.

You is the second most spoken English word

In New Jersey, it's illegal to wear a bulletproof vest while committing a violent crime.

Elephants think people are cute, the same way people think puppies or kittens are cute.

Salt used to be a currency.

Apple paid a couple $1.7 million dollars for their plot of land, which was only worth $181,700.

September 3rd is International Bacon Day.

The useful life of a modern toilet is about 50 years.

Antimatter is the most expensive substance on earth. It costs roughly $62.5 trillion per gram, or $1.75 quadrillion per ounce.

The horn of a rhinoceros is made from compacted hair rather than bone or another substance.

November 17th is known as "Unfriend Day". On this day you should unfriend anybody who you don't know or speak to.

The tongue is the only muscle in one's body that is attached from one end.

The penguin is the only bird that can swim but can't fly.

Dr. Seuss invented the word "nerd."

Soviet Russia needed lighthouses on their uninhabited Northern Coast, so they built automated lighthouses powered by small nuclear reactors.

The word
"Android" means a human with a male robot appearance.

There are times when Pluto is closer to the Sun than Neptune - one of these timelines was from 1979 to 1999.

Batman and Predator exist in the same fictional universe. Since 1991, they have been featured together in three comic books.

On average, 46.1% of Americans have less than $10,000 in assets when they die.

Most pandas in the world are on loan from China.

Every person has a unique tongue print.

Al Capone's business card said he was a used furniture dealer.

Facebook pays at least $500 if you can find a way to hack the site.

July 3rd is International Plastic Bag Free Day - it's a day about making a little change to make a big impact (for the better) in the future.

Music has some pretty interesting effects on living things - It makes plants grow faster and cows produce more milk.

Insects such as bees, mosquitoes and cicadas make noise by rapidly moving their wings.

A dog was the first living creature to be sent into space in 1957.

15% of iPhone users use an iPhone with a broken screen.

Drink green tea before bed to burn calories while sleeping. Green tea will also increase your metabolism.

28 is the atomic number of Nickel, and the atomic mass of Silicon.

The first 4th of July celebration was in 1777.

Egg yolks are one of the few foods that naturally contain Vitamin D.

The average person in France sleeps 8.83 hours per day, the most in the developed world.

Abraham Lincoln loved cats and once let one eat from the table during a formal White House dinner.

Zebras have only one toe on each foot.

The only 15-letter word that can be spelled without repeating a letter is uncopyrightable.

There was once an undersea post office in the Bahamas.

Sugar was first added to chewing gum in 1869 by a dentist, William Semple.

During 1922 & 1933, The Coca-Cola Company was offered a chance to buy the Pepsi-Cola company, and it declined on three separate occasions.

Foxes have whiskers on their legs. This helps them with their bearings, especially when it's dark outside.

There are 31,557,600 seconds in a year.

Every 10 years, the human skeleton repairs and renews itself. Essentially, you have different bones now than you did 10 years ago!

People who donate blood in Sweden are sent a text message each time their blood saves a life.

A female heart is smaller than a male heart by about 25%.

Both Motel 6 and Super 8 got their names from the original prices of the rooms. Motel 6 started at $6 in 1962, and Super 8 at $8.88 in 1974.

There are 3900 islands in the country Japan, the country of islands.

In general, people tend to read as much as 10% slower from a screen than from paper.

Some butterfly species are extremely fast; the Skipper Butterfly can fly faster than a horse can run.

Finland has the most metal bands per capita.

A giraffe can clean its ears with its 21-inch tongue!

Ancient Roman surgeons were trained to block out the screams of human pain.

"Strategic incompetence" is the art of avoiding certain tasks by pretending you don't know how to do them.

In a human foot there are 26 bones.

Jennifer Lopez was the first actress to have a movie and an album hit number one in the same week.

Canadians say "sorry" so much that a law was passed in 2009 declaring that an apology can't be used as evidence of admission to guilt.

Sour Patch Kids are from the same manufacturer as Swedish Fish. The red Sour Patch Kids are the same candy as Swedish Fish, but with sour sugar.

In Japan, many families eat a KFC for Christmas Dinner. Many people order their meals months in advance and queue for hours to collect them.

Rabbits can be literally "scared to death" if approached by a predator when they are totally unaware.

Space is completely, totally, and utterly silent.

The average life expectancy of a toucan is a very impressive 20 years.

A pig's orgasm lasts for 30 minutes.

A woman faked her entire tragedy and the loss of her husband during the 9/11 attacks and became President of the Support Network in New York.

It's not just humans who are right or left-handed. Most female cats prefer using their right paw and males are more likely to be left-pawed.

Garrett McNamara holds the record for the largest wave ever surfed, set in 2011 in Nazare, Portugal. The wave was 78 feet tall.

The name ASOS is an acronym for "As Seen On Screen"

Enceladus, one of Saturn's smaller moons, reflects 90% of the sunlight, making it more reflective than snow.

Before finally being accepted, J.K. Rowling's original Harry Potter pitch was rejected by 12 publishers.

The Hobbit has been published in two editions. In the first edition, Gollum willingly bet on his ring in the riddle game.

The average person spends six months of their lifetime waiting for a red light to turn green.

Hard cheeses have a longer shelf live than soft cheeses.

Madagascar once was a stomping ground for lemurs which were the size of today's gorillas.

India has over 50 million monkeys.

Disney World is the second-largest purchaser of explosives in the United States, the first being the U.S. Department of Defense.

Slinkies are 82 feet long.

There are 923 words in the English language that break the "I before E" rule. Only 44 words actually follow that rule.

While watching a Merry-Go-Round from a bench in Griffith Park, Los Angeles, Walt Disney was struck with inspiration for the creation of Disneyland.

Mount Rushmore cost less than one million dollars to construct. It took 14 years to build - from 1927 to 1941, and took 400 workers.

The human brain is about 75% water.

The Ethiopian calendar is 7.5 years behind the Gregorian calendar due to the fact that it has 13 months.

It takes Uranus 84 years to orbit the Sun once.

Giant Arctic jellyfish have tentacles that can reach over 36 metres in length.

COORDINATION

B	H	E	A	Y	F	H	B	T	C	I	R	F	W	I
X	C	T	N	Z	F	B	K	R	O	J	M	X	D	V
T	O	E	E	O	S	Z	E	J	L	Y	O	P	G	J
V	H	R	J	O	E	E	G	U	L	C	J	A	E	D
O	E	C	G	N	S	W	H	N	A	O	J	R	Y	B
I	R	N	P	O	I	J	W	I	B	U	L	T	D	Y
F	E	O	E	I	C	Z	R	S	O	R	E	N	Y	C
I	N	C	F	T	N	Y	D	F	R	T	P	E	N	O
Q	T	Q	C	A	O	G	E	E	A	E	A	R	W	M
X	A	V	C	R	C	R	Z	H	T	O	Q	S	K	M
B	L	X	L	E	M	E	Q	Y	I	U	Y	H	W	U
X	L	G	E	P	B	N	A	M	O	S	T	I	D	N
E	T	Y	A	O	G	Y	E	I	N	I	I	P	O	I
Z	C	Q	R	O	O	S	L	N	R	M	N	Z	G	T
G	O	K	I	C	T	Q	S	M	P	M	U	L	Z	Y

CLEAR	CONCRETE	UNITY
COHERENT	COOPERATION	
COLLABORATION	COURTEOUS	
COMMUNITY	PARTNERSHIP	
CONCISE	SYNERGY	

COORDINATION
Puzzle # 1

		E						C					
	C	T						O					
	O	E						L			P		
	H	R			E			L	C		A		
	E	C		N	S			A	O		R		
	R	N		O	I			B	U		T		
	E	O		I	C			O	R		N		C
	N	C		T	N	Y		R	T		E		O
	T			A	O	G		A	E		R		M
			C	R	C	R		T	O		S		M
			L	E		E		I	U	Y	H		U
			E	P		N		O	S	T	I		N
			A	O		Y		N		I	P		I
			R	O		S				N			T
				C						U			Y

1.

BON PHRKEN CYKMB KC PXHN BW CBPU PKFXWFEN MWF WLNF 6 VWEBOC YKBOWSB BWSQOKET AWYE.

. . . .

2.

NYXP TZRG Z SYSZF YU 42 SGGST ETGD STGC ZAG UMFFC-XAYED.

. . . .

3.

G YKRKLE BCADRE RZGLV AGJ MK 460 RIDGLK VOBKR OJ ROWK GJY AGJ ACJRDVK 423 VOBBOCJ TCDJYR CS TBGJER OJ G ROJUBK YGQ.

. . . .

4.

UJEF KQDRLN WJJGE'N WIJGELI JFZL NVSLY GEL DQHL JH VWIVEVO DQFZJDF'N NJF.

. . . .

5.

DPQ EAAG ZU MOUD 27% DPQ UZCQ AN DPQ QFBDP.

. . . .

6.

MBWJ EHNX PEUXX JXPJ MK XQXWRFJ.

. . . .

7.

KZAPRX GKZQ XGF UESR EJ XGF MPNZH KNF CFUX IO

QKNAFNR EJ LGEJK.

. . . .

8.

WCZTL MALHMLXN WHQL XCVOARB 85% CK MALTX

DXCKTM CKK YCUYLNNTCU NMHUEN. MATN TN SLYHVNL

MTYQLM XLZLUVLN AHZL MC SL NAHXLE PTMA MAL

WCZTL ETNMXTSVMCXN.

. . . .

9.

JYKKCFY OZ KLY HETJQZ GEZK RERCJPT VTYYM
AYVYKPUJY.

. . . .
10.

YCG IAMB MGYYGO YCKY QIGPA'Y KXXGKO IA YCG
XGODIQDZ YKHMG DP U.

. . . .
11.

KXJKEIN JQXIK 'RCGQQ KRXGK' HI PDGQXI. RCHK
TXK BCDKQI SM RCQ ZDEIYQG SQBXEKQ CQ
TXIRQY RCQ BDJOXIM RD SQ ODTQGZEF XIY
QWQGFXKRHIN FHPQ KRXGK HI RCQ KPM.

. . . .
12.

HREVBOMV FCP MJ JNOVK TRQ HRRVJXMVC. MB POJ
RQMKMVONNZ SQCOBCF OJ O HMACQ TRQ HRRVJXMVC OVF
PXMJWCZ MV BCVVCJJCC.

. . . .

13.

BRDEAP IBEJX, MNX BVDRP   PVAG.

. . . .

14.

IXIJP ZIJYMB WHY H   GBQTGI KMBDGI ZJQBK.

. . . .

15.

YJDWHOUYHP JECU 3 VHUP   HW UEOJ THHV.

. . . .

16.

IXK UMKSWUX VWIF BH UIBVGXBNT WU DCWNI

YVLBUU 14 SWHHKLKEI WUNYESU.

. . . .

17.

PYL BYWAPLBP KNRL EYLRZENX LXLRLKP ZK
PYL DLAZWTZE PNMXL WV LXLRLKPB ZB PZK.

. . . .
18.

E TCEDZYKQJ OEY KQJ EA   40LRX (25BRX).

. . . .
19.

WAXNWA QOEZKRWIXR, IZA BKNEI JE TNAEKLARI,
RAHAN CKHAL OI IZA QZKIA ZXJEA.

. . . .
20.

CPN QJZB IJCP CPN LZNYCNTC IJMLTDYM JT
CPN IYMBNZJML YGQYCZSTT YC RD CS 11.8 HC (3.63
E).

. . . .

21.

NWGPR FPFULD POL FXOR KUJN 300 FXRLD. PEWMJD
NPQL 206 FXRLD FLBPWDL GPRZ XS JNXDL 300 FXRLD
KL POL FXOR KUJN SWDL JXHLJNLO.

. . . .
22.

QYF WJYOPF LFVWKQQY QB AQYFU HFKHFWFYLW LAF
PJBF XQHE QB 12 GFFW.

. . . .
23.

ULQ RNUOTHL TN ULQ USGGQNU MTOZ TX ULQ
IROGZ. TU HSX VORI JC UR 9 PQQU USGG.

. . . .
24.

LKRWR HWR HWIBTX 16 AZMMZIT FRIFMR HMZYR
LIXHJ LKHL HWR XZWRGL XROGRTXHTLO IV DRTDKZO
SKHT.

. . . .

25.

LAT HKKLYFEULM WPGT KU LAT WKKU JERR VT LATFT
HKF 100 WERREKU STPFM.

. . . .

26.

FZMRFQEMD GFOYZXPQ BFT TGPX FQE OPDXFZZW
BPHQEME LW FFDPQ LHDD PQ XGM TFOM TUPX XGFX
GYT TPQ GFE LMMQ AYZZME 3 WMFDT LMSPDM, FQE LW
XGM TFOM TMX PS UYTXPZT.

. . . .

27.

TXQPLCQ AMBXFM, PCZMRA MYV CRMHBV QL QMAQV
DLLO.

. . . .

28.

QDGU MBMAPRFUG EMTVP BMGG UPRF UPM UDFVKM
DW R YBKM EPRBM.

. . . .

29.

LIR GZ GQRPK QPMQ ZPC DZEGREG YEL CZFRK
FYGRK DZEGREG, TPOGYDQPZO YKR TKZER GZ
ORCS-QRYGPEM. PE SYDG, PS GKYEOTZKGRL PE CYKMR
MKZITO, GQRA DYE OTZEGYERZIOCA DZBHIOG.

. . . .
30.

RCVWBIRKVC VWROIHL ZBW TRUGOIA R CQRYH FX
TRUGOIA VSWBKAS CTOJJOIA QBBUC THRWOIA
VSHOW CQRYH CKOVC.

. . . .
31.

M NBRWQBPPBN NQBMLQ-LMUPBH YML'N
LMUP WMV YB PBVILQBVBH GZ NQGZLBVBH HTZUVI
APUIQL.

. . . .
32.

DGBJLCRJ BJO ZYIRK LS KDBCZI GLLH KLGYW,
BJOX DZO DEBCDGGX NDWO CT SZLN NYGGYLIK LS
EGCNTK LS YEO DIW ZLEH.

. . . .

33.

NDTZUJPBQMI TN Q BQMIBEOYJI OEKMZPL QMI
LJZ NZTBB AQN Q MQFL DTZA 10 NATXN.

. . . .

34.

LBEYMH YSFZHYSF JLP RLZHYMYP GLBGCBCZ EN
HJY HYFPYM LAY QO 15.

. . . .

35.

LWYUY EUY DXYU 6,000 MKDOK GNYFSYG DV
AUEGG.

. . . .

36.

RKGLRLIIPLO HPKK EFV IPYLE GEVPK VTLD BIL
YPNSLA.

. . . .

37.

WX QTX QCUGKJ GOGK BHOG QBG JHZG JQKCSGJ, HWP
QBCJ CJ BXT CWPCOCPAHR QCUGKJ MHW FG
CPGWQCLCGP.

. . . .
38.

YQ MAQCKPMI, YC YL YEEAFRE CJ PRDDI
YPA-PDARH YQ IJKD URPM NJPMAC.

. . . .
39.

VZELWA CMEBV CXE LL, XFGELTXWN SELGV SM
SEXLW IXSN SM VEMD IMFIN.

. . . .
40.

GRGLOIESF OIWG SOG RIZHGFS TZIKE BD IEN
VIVVIR; SOGKZ TZIKEF AGKHO IE IWGZIHG BD 11
LBMEJF.

. . . .

41.

YURL NFYYGRZMGBP KDHSGHK YGZBUQH UBJFRP 500
YGOHK HUSN LHUB.

. . . .
42.

YUKUKUI UFC FUERVUGLRNC.

. . . .
43.

NHQAIFWIA FHSQAL SPEGWYAB FE IANAP
YRHNA HXHWI WZ HJPHRHG QWIUEQI OHY AQAUFAB
SPAYWBAIF. RA BWAB WI 1910 OWFR H
12-ZEEF-QEIX JAHPB.

. . . .
44.

QVLG FER BFEOFJWWG HFE'A SFDB YFHBSFJRG.

. . . .

45.

AYX ETRVXNA HGSHPXA AXNA BWAHY EWNAXK TUXG 12
KWZN QXAOXXR XRVEWRK WRK NTJAY WDGSHW. SA
TREZ XRKXK QXHWJNX AYX XRVESNY AXWB OTJEK YWUX
BSNNXK AYXSG QTWA YTBX.

. . . .
46.

SGSGV AYVLN KWJDC PGQCD AVSCYHWV VLU CGGCD
UYSVE.

. . . .
47.

ATK LWCKGACOCW AKFJ OYF VFPCG OFKKQK CL
'LRTKGYRPHPACGK UPGUHCYGKNFPHUCP'.

. . . .
48.

H 'GQTJKI' TP HJ TJOHUTXHJX QD GKKBP TJ
AQILPOTIK.

. . . .

49.

J GOJBB JOLWYI LP JBHLTLB NBJHUQ LY J

GHLMNELY REBB OJAU EI KL HMJXS JYQ GIEYK

EIGUBP IL QUJIT.

. . . .

50.

ALJE JKSQYHJ ZROY EHRIJKRHYIE TXLLQ.

. . . .

51.

IDO WVJI IGFCGISHO RSXU SP IDO LVXFU SJ IDO

GAXSQGP YXGM EGXXVI. SI QGP JGM VHOX 800 LVXUJ

LDSFO WVJI VIDOX JEOQSOJ VA EGXXVIJ QGP

FOGXP VPFM 50.

. . . .

52.

GXGW XB ULW JWZUIWF SXNIR KWZR QNFPS.

. . . .

53.

URRWSFYIUNQET 1/3 SJ NXQ BSWEHL SBE LRQMYQL UWQ
QYNXQW QGHUGDQWQH SW UN WYLV.

. . . .

54.

IJCYZH TBTJR 250,000 RTIJD EKT AIWZTEQL
ZCJEK IZH DCYEK NCXTD UQXX DUQELK NCXIJQER.

. . . .

55.

YNS EWQHSK RQ RFYKWQRCY OF OQ FMRVS YNS DSRISK
YNSOK ZWQSF ZSVWTS.

. . . .

56.

CHB EHKZTW 80% HE LFVW CHB JTVKY TVDF AVC.

. . . .

57.

YEM DNLJQJL KLMNH JP YEM ZKCXW'P WMMDMPY.

. . . .

58.

F PQI SFG ZVT WCXGZ BCUCEI MXTFZOXT ZQ NT

GTEZ CEZQ GKFMT CE 1957.

. . . .

59.

HWCR SYJL GLLU ORLX GQ PSL TWIWPYBQ.

. . . .

60.

DCA QBMAYD JKQEK YQHU WATXUA MSDAY ISTJ DQ

6,000 I.T. DCA XKZWAMXAKDY XKTBHMAM

CXUUQUQDSPHY SKM YUSWWQE PASD.

. . . .

61.

SKMGAUXBR VMU BUKO JMC FACT CTJAQ TJMZR
PWRAZJ ZBFU.

. . . .
62.

SXSLFWRHVQXEJFERWS WY MOSX EM JOSPHV RHVVOX
YVWLCWPK VE VFO XEEM EM QEHX DEHVF.

. . . .
63.

QGDCFFSWQ KBE KWCJI NFSSQ XBQNSF NABE NASO
KBE FDE UE NAS LFUDEV.

. . . .
64.

GJKCDY CSHBYCSH XGB OGDDSCE YA QSB ESBYGHY
FAZBSH; CJBG CSHBYCSH.

. . . .

65.

DEIIZIU JGVVXIV SIYI KYGOGZREEH GZJIZPIP
AKY ORV BRVDV.

. . . .
66.

IRR BSRLEQ LX SXEYFXIESLXIR MRSUWEQ
SHYXESMK EWYDQYRTYQ SX YXURSQW FYUIFHRYQQ LM
EWYSF NLAXEFK LM LFSUSX.

. . . .
67.

R PBLRCB ABRYW KZ ZLRCCBY WARD R LRCB
ABRYW MI RMFTW 25%.

. . . .
68.

JO 1937, B WBNGA SJAV FAGTV GEM BM MZV SGH
SJXW QMECJGQ JO OVK NVAQVR. MZV SJAV
CVQMAGRVC 75% GS MZVJA WGLJVQ, JOPXECJOD WGQM
GS MZVJA QJXVOM SJXWQ.

. . . .

69.

CRWO JBRJGB WLBE 40 GPW (16.14 XY) RI WXDZ DZ
N GDIBODCB.

. . . .
70.

W RGMSQWH ZFTWK YFR QIKRWSKN WOIFR IKL
ZFKJALJ RASHHSIK OWQRLASWH QLHHN.

. . . .
71.

Y BTPKQ EOSMJU YHPKIQ Y GSTTSPI XPIU.

. . . .
72.

NFXSKOOYXMJI JUDIKUKO COKG UX NKFSXFL YM
QJCGKQYIIK GCFYMP UDK XSS-OKJOXM.

. . . .

73.

JMSYI PG IYJ IJR WLESJOI OILIQJO MR IYJ CPEWN
LEJ PG DQNNYL'O.

. . . .

74.

IDTCMMQ BQCTAR ZYHZ ANDXQ CR BCTP CR C
XFN'R BQCTA, DE FTPQT AF IQA KOFFP AF DAR
KTCDE.

. . . .

75.

QSZEUKZQ ASZKJQ YKSYBK JZK BKVJBBI SQBI
JBBSMKL ES UJPK SQK SX 28 UJHZDOEW. RKQ JQL
MSRKQ DJQ DUSSWK XZSR 14 LHXXKZKQE WEIBKW.

. . . .

76.

SUZF EUR LBRJ ZGHBY LXXJ BR ZXZUW JUYTRHFF.

. . . .

77.

ZKMSM VSM 132 SQQDB CI ZKM EB HKCZM KQEBM.

. . . .

78.

WA TDBCJGWJ, XRLXBR QMJHR KMRWG MRJPQ KL

WAPWZJKR 'NRQ' JAP ALP OLG 'AL'.

. . . .

79.

GF 1942, ZDJCJ XHP H LHF GF LGPPGPPGRRG WHKKJB

ZDJ RDHFZVL YHCYJC XDV XVTKB YCJHA GFZV

RJVRKJ'P DVTPJP HZ FGSDZ HFB WTZ ZDJGC

DHGC.

. . . .

80.

POM ZHMNMPXC XQ TC TQYLVTC MNMDOTCP

TVVXWCPZ QXY TKXWP 15% XQ LPZ KXEJ FMLSOP.

. . . .

1: B=T
2: S=T
3: R=S
4: L=E
5: D=T
6: J=S
7: F=E
8: M=T
9: K=T
10: Y=T
11: K=S
12: C=E
13: R=E
14: B=N
15: U=E
16: W=I
17: P=T
18: X=H
19: I=T
20: Y=A
21: P=A
22: Q=O
23: Q=E
24: H=A
25: K=O
26: M=E
27: Q=T
28: P=H
29: R=E
30: O=I
31: L=T
32: D=A
33: N=S
34: L=A
35: U=R
36: P=I
37: C=I
38: A=E
39: L=I
40: G=E
41: U=A
42: C=E
43: H=A
44: E=N
45: A=T
46: G=O
47: C=I
48: J=N

49: L=O
50: R=A
51: G=A
52: X=O
53: W=R
54: E=T
55: R=A
56: H=O
57: J=I
58: Z=T
59: W=I
60: D=T
61: J=E
62: V=T
63: E=N
64: C=E
65: V=S
66: Y=E
67: B=E
68: J=I
69: D=I
70: K=N
71: Y=A
72: X=O

73: I=T
74: T=R
75: S=O
76: R=N
77: K=H
78: J=A
79: J=E
80: P=T

1.

The Alpine Swift is able to stay airborne for over 6 months without touching down.

2.

Dogs have a total of 42 teeth when they are fully-grown.

3.

A desert locust swarm can be 460 square miles in size and can consume 423 million pounds of plants in a single day.

4.

John Wilkes Booth's brother once saved the life of Abraham Lincoln's son.

5.

The moon is just 27% the size of the earth.

6.

Owls Have Three Sets of Eyelids.

7.

Almost half the pigs in the world are kept by

farmers in China.

8.

Movie theaters make roughly 85% of their

profit off concession stands. This is because

ticket revenues have to be shared with the

movie distributors.

9.

Lettuce is the worlds most popular green vegetable.

10.

The only letter that doesn't appear on the periodic table is J.

11.

Samsung means 'three stars' in Korean. This was chosen by the founder because he wanted the company to be powerful and everlasting like stars in the sky.

12.

Mountain Dew is slang for moonshine. It was originally created as a mixer for moonshine and whiskey in Tennessee.

13.

Lemons float, but limes sink.

14.

Every person has a unique tongue print.

15.

Rhinoceros have 3 toes on each foot.

16.

The Swedish city of Stockholm is built

across 14 different islands.

17.

The shortest name chemical element in

the periodic table of elements is tin.

18.

A dragonfly can fly at 40kph (25mph).

19.

George Washington, the first US president,

never lived at the White House.

20.

The bird with the greatest wingspan is

the Wandering Albatross at up to 11.8 ft (3.63

m).

21.

Human babies are born with 300 bones. Adults
have 206 bones because many of those 300 bones
we are born with fuse together.

22.

One single teaspoon of honey represents the
life work of 12 bees.

23.

The ostrich is the tallest bird in the
world. It can grow up to 9 feet tall.

24.

There are around 16 million people alive
today that are direct descendants of Genghis
Khan.

25.

The footprints made on the moon will be there for 100 million years.

26.

Alexander Hamilton was shot and mortally wounded by Aaron Burr on the same spot that his son had been killed 3 years before, and by the same set of pistols.

27.

Without saliva, humans are unable to taste food.

28.

Most elephants weigh less than the tongue of a blue whale.

29.

Due to their high oil content and lower water content, pistachios are prone to self-heating. In fact, if transported in large groups, they can spontaneously combust.

30.

Astronauts trained for walking a space by walking through swimming pools wearing their space suits.

31.

A Seychelles Sheath-Tailed Bat's tail can be lengthened or shortened during flight.

32.

Although the rings of Saturn look solid, they are actually made up from millions of clumps of ice and rock.

33.

Switzerland is a landlocked country and yet still has a Navy with 10 ships.

34.

Albert Einstein had mastered calculus by the tender age of 15.

35.

There are over 6,000 known species of grass.

36.

Blueberries will not ripen until they are picked.

37.

No two tigers ever have the same stripes, and this is how individual tigers can be identified.

38.

In Kentucky, it is illegal to carry ice-cream in your back pocket.

39.

During World War II, Americans tried to train bats to drop bombs.

40.

Elephants have the largest brain of any mammal; their brains weigh an average of 11 pounds.

41.

Many hummingbird species migrate around 500

miles each year.

42.

Bananas are radioactive.

43.

Valentine Tapley promised to never

shave again if Abraham Lincoln was elected

president. He died in 1910 with a

12-foot-long beard.

44.

Emus and kangaroos can't walk backwards.

45.

The longest Cricket Test match lasted over 12

days between England and South Africa. It

only ended because the English team would have

missed their boat home.

46.

Cocoa beans fight mouth bacteria and tooth

decay.

47.

The scientific term for brain freeze is

'sphenopalatine ganglioneuralgia'.

48.

A 'Loiner' is an inhabitant of Leeds in

Yorkshire.

49.

A small amount of alcohol placed on a
scorpion will make it go crazy and sting
itself to death.

50.

Most spiders have transparent blood.

51.

The most talkative bird in the world is the
African gray parrot. It can say over 800 words
while most other species of parrots can
learn only 50.

52.

None of The Beatles could read music.

53.

Approximately 1/3 of the worlds owl species are either endangered or at risk.

54.

Around every 250,000 years the magnetic North and South poles will switch polarity.

55.

The longer an astronaut is in space the weaker their bones become.

56.

You forget 80% of what you learn each day.

57.

The Pacific Ocean is the world's deepest.

58.

A dog was the first living creature to be

sent into space in 1957.

59.

Pigs have been used by the military.

60.

The oldest known soup recipe dates back to

6,000 B.C. The ingredients included

hippopotamus and sparrow meat.

61.

Flamingos can only eat with their heads

upside down.

62.

Arachibutyrophobia is fear of peanut butter

sticking to the roof of your mouth.

63.

Squirrels can climb trees faster than they

can run on the ground.

64.

Albert Einstein was married to his distant

cousin; Elsa Einstein.

65.

Kleenex tissues were originally intended
for gas masks.

66.

All pilots on international flights
identify themselves in English regardless of
their country of origin.

67.

A female heart is smaller than a male
heart by about 25%.

68.

In 1937, a major fire broke out at the Fox
Film studios in New Jersey. The fire
destroyed 75% of their movies, including most
of their silent films.

69.

Most people shed 40 lbs (16.14 kg) of skin in

a lifetime.

70.

A typical human gut contains about one

hundred trillion bacterial cells.

71.

A cloud weighs around a million tons.

72.

Professional athletes used to perform in

vaudeville during the off-season.

73.

Eight of the ten largest statues in the world
are of Buddha's.

74.

Giraffe hearts pump twice as hard as a
cow's heart, in order to get blood to its
brain.

75.

Northern Korean people are legally only
allowed to have one of 28 haircuts. Men and
women can choose from 14 different styles.

76.

Bats can find their food in total darkness.

77.

There are 132 rooms in the US White House.

78.

In Bulgaria, people shake their heads to

indicate 'yes' and nod for 'no'.

79.

In 1942, there was a man in Mississippi called

the Phantom Barber who would break into

people's houses at night and cut their

hair.

80.

The skeleton of an African elephant

accounts for about 15% of its body weight.